The
D'Artagnan
Way

...a Tale of Purpose, Passion, & Team Commitment

FOR KATRINA

INSPIRE YOUR TEAM THE
D'ARTAGNAN WAY! ALL TIK
BEST.

Harvey

The D'Artagnan Way: A Tale of Purpose, Passion & Team Commitment
by Harvey A. Meier and Larry A. Bauman

Published by Columba Publishing Company, Inc.
Akron, OH USA
Copyright 2005 Harvey A. Meier and Larry A. Bauman
All rights reserved
Manufactured in the United States of America
ISBN 0-938655-78-7

Editor
Sheri L. Galat

10 9 8 7 6 5 4 3 2 1

Cover photograph by Harvey A. Meier

The
D'Artagnan
Way

...a Tale of Purpose, Passion, & Team Commitment

by
Harvey A. Meier
Larry A. Bauman

COLUMBA PUBLISHING COMPANY, INC.
AKRON, OHIO   44313   USA

Authors' Acknowledgements

To all of those who have inspired me in a positive and con-
structive way to practice the principles of the D'Artagnan
Way in my personal and business life—to my wife, Susan,
and to my children, Sascha and Sabrina; to my parents, Betty
and Morris and to my friends and business associates, Gary,
Bill, Claude, Mary, Bill, Hans, John, Tom, Mike, Dan,
Harvey, Clint, Lew, Dennis, Phil, Beth, Bob, Dick, Marvin,
Bernie, Jennifer, Claus, Pat, and Larry.
　　—HARVEY

To all those who have allowed me to find my way, the
D'Artagnan Way, by offering support to pursue those dreams
and be the best at whatever I choose to do. This is for my
family, Beth, Blair and Brad, friends, and colleagues. Each
of you knows who you are. You all mean more to me than
you will ever know.

And to Harvey, without whose profound beliefs, continuing
guidance, and constant friendship, this book would have
never become a reality. Life is short and the joy is in the
ride. Enjoy every minute.
　　—LARRY

What People are Saying About 'The D'Artagnan Way':

"*The D'Artagnan Way* is a great parable that focuses on your most important resource—your people. In a few pages the story gives you important principles to leverage your company's personnel assets."
Grant Lundberg, CEO
Lundberg Family Farms

"*The D'Artagnan Way* provides a very strong visual of how people from various cultures, opposite mindsets, and different interests can work together as a team when everyone agrees with a common goal or objective."
Fred Rodgers, Executive Vice President
Pfingsten Publishing LLC

"Meier and Bauman present powerful material that any organization, executive team, or individual can put to practical use immediately."
Robert Lowy, Executive Director of Human Resources
Stevens Health Care

"Meier and Bauman have crafted a modern-day parable that provides many useful messages for any type of organization—in an industry or university setting. The story makes for an interesting read, and is chock-full of take-home messages for managers and other leaders."
John Foltz, Professor of Agribusiness Management and Associate Dean, University of Idaho

Table of Contents

SECTION ONE
Introduction

Introduction

Whether companies continue to fight through the economic downturn or emerge triumphant into another round of boom times, one question remains crucial for business leaders: How can we inspire our workforce and bring out the best in our employees and in ourselves?

Motivating employees and ourselves to be passionate about and committed to our work and our personal lives is a key strategy for achieving success in many organizations; inspired workers and leaders can achieve greatness. Companies and organizations need to create a team of committed, passionate, and inspired players if they are going to not only survive, but thrive in future years.

This book is written specifically for business leaders that depend on teamwork, passion, and inspiration to outperform their competitors and achieve organizational goals and, perhaps, even greatness.

Leaders and employees who are masters of their own motivation and who are able to "keep their eyes on the prize," regardless of the vagaries of their industry or the nation's economic conditions, will consistently outperform their peers. Across the country, business leaders know this and invest millions of dollars in motivational training for themselves and for their employees.

However, almost everyone agrees that the effects of motivational training are usually short-lived. Leaders and employees need more than just motivational training—they need inspiration, inspiration that can be tapped into beyond the classroom or auditorium setting, in the privacy of their own hearts and minds. An enduring aspiration to greatness does not spring from gimmicky programs with toys and doodads tossed to training participants as if they were seals performing for fish. This aspiration feeds on a deep well of understanding that allows them to say, "I belong to a purpose greater than myself, and I am not alone in this journey. I can draw from the support, talent, and expertise of my closest circle."

Much emphasis has been placed upon motivation as a catalyst for success in organization performance, but there is little discussion of the inspiration that drives business leaders and employees—unless that inspiration has come from religious messages, which have a variety of obvious drawbacks in the corporate setting.

Still, the use of an allegory in religious messages has long been recognized as a powerful way to influence and shift thinking toward a loftier vision of what is possible. *The D'Artagnan Way—A Tale of Purpose, Passion, and Team Commitment*, is a non-religious allegory that updates the noble principles of a different kind of inspiring saga: *The Three Musketeers*. It is presented in the spirit of *Who Moved*

My Cheese, The Go-Getter, The One-Minute Manager, and numerous other successful business allegories which serve as influential agents of change inside organizations.

Set in the modern day upscale (and fictional) coastal village of Esperanza, *The D'Artagnan Way* introduces us to the transforming powers of a famous principle: "All for One, One for All." Esperanza serves as a metaphor for all companies and organizations in American business striving to survive the economic turmoil of the last several years while keeping their vision for the future alive and relevant.

As the story opens, Esperanza is about to fall on hard times, causing the community of long-time friends to estrange themselves from each other, competing for whatever bit of opportunity might come their way. In the midst of these bad times they are presented with an unexpected challenge that requires them to pull together and trust one another in order to bring about success. They make progress only when they set aside their competitiveness and become a committed team united by their goal.

The catalyst for this change is a young stranger named Jim D'Artagnan (dar-tanion), modeled after the passionate, idealistic fourth Musketeer in "The Three Musketeers," written by French author Alexandre Dumas more than two centuries ago. Beloved for generations for the exuberant rallying cry: "All for one, one for all!" the Dumas story dramatizes and celebrates the heroic virtues of that era: teamwork; devotion to excellence; sacrifice; trust; generosity of heart and spirit; and the most powerful virtue of all—firm dedication to a cause greater than oneself. We call these noble, team-oriented principles "The D'Artagnan Way."

Young Jim D'Artagnan carries his name proudly and draws inspiration from this family gift, even in the modern day world. Unlike the 18th century D'Artagnan, Jim has no royalty to protect, but his 21st century cause is even greater: the environment, especially the graceful dolphins that play up and down the U.S. shores. As his story unfolds, Jim D'Artagnan and the townspeople of Esperanza are inspired to follow the principles of the D'Artagnan Way, serving a goal far greater than their individual needs and concerns.

In the challenging world we confront each day, many uncertainties impact each of us. How we choose to deal with these circumstances—and the people involved—creates the world we live in and the successes that result. Choosing to be involved is personal; choosing to involve others is critical. Whether dealing with difficulties in the face of terrorism, or the challenge of saving an animal, the choices we make drive our inner being and can provide compelling examples for others to follow.

WHAT IS THE D'ARTAGNAN WAY?

The D'Artagnan Way is the inspired practice of unselfish teamwork and collaboration, based on a foundation of truth, honor, and integrity.

To put the D'Artagnan Way into action, we must visualize belonging to a purpose greater than ourselves. We must believe we are not alone in our career and life's journey. And we must put aside self-interest and commit to self-sacrifice and teamwork for a larger cause—a greater mission.

The principles of the Musketeer motto, "All for One, One for All," are the key lessons of our story. They are presented at the end of this book as teachable principles.

PRINCIPLES OF THE D'ARTAGNAN WAY

- Commit to a Shared Dream
- Create Strategic Alliances
- Respect Each Other's Differences
- Maintain a Positive Attitude
- Choose to Trust
- Do the Right Thing
- Celebrate Success

Section Two
A Tale of Purpose, Passion, & Team Commitment

Chapter One

For many years the small seaside village of Esperanza was a
very cheerful place. Tucked into a crescent embraced by
lush, green mountains on one side and a clear, tropical bay
on the other, Esperanza welcomed families, golfers, honey-
mooners, and artists to its streets, shops, and sandy white
beaches. Windows were framed with boxes of luxuriant red
geraniums, and parking spaces were marked not by parking
meters, but by huge tubs of pansies, daisies, and day lilies.
Bougainvilleas climbed gleaming white stucco walls, and hot
pink fuchsias dripped from colorful pots hanging from the
branches of thriving cypress trees.

In the mornings golfers would convene at the world-class
courses overlooking the crashing surf, while shoppers
explored delightful shops selling gold and diamonds, Italian
pottery, and linens from Provence. Out on the bay, boaters
hoisted their sails, watching the colorful canvas billowing in
fresh breezes, sea-washed during their long journey across the

ocean from Asia. After sumptuous lunches of fresh seafood served over homemade pasta, everyone took their favorite books down to the beach, where the children would play in the soft white sand, digging and building various shapes.

By the end of the day, when the last of the visitors left the sunset-tinted beach, sandcastles, sand birthday cakes, and sand mermaids dotted the landscape. By morning, as the sun came up over the mountaintops, the beach would be washed clean again by the ocean, ready for another day of tourists.

Yes, all the visitors agreed, Esperanza was a most enchanting place to be. How wonderful it would be to actually live there full-time. They came from around the world and would spend hours over congenial drinks at the Firebird Bar enjoying its friendly, relaxed atmosphere while marveling at the beauty of the beach. And every night, long after the last visitor had gone to bed, many of the Esperanza merchants would meet at the Firebird to celebrate the successes of the day.

"I sold out of my new shipment of shirts the very first day!" said Dave, the T-shirt storekeeper.

"I need to lay in a whole new order of sunblock to restock my shelves," called out Tom, the drugstore owner.

"I'm booked solid through Labor Day," exclaimed Phyllis, the Starfish Bed and Breakfast innkeeper.

"All my boats are chartered until Thanksgiving," said Sam, the marina owner.

And best of all, they agreed, they were busier than Concurso, their rival village 75 miles south. Congratulating themselves and each other, they lifted their glasses to toast the prosperous summer they anticipated ahead of them. After all, this was only April, and they were already off to a fantastic start!

One person in the bar didn't share their excitement. Blair Spratley was a local girl who had saved the money she made making hotel beds every year to buy the Firebird Bar from her old friend and mentor, Ike, who 40 years earlier had made beds to buy the bar from an old fisherman, Carl.

Blair spent her early mornings drinking steaming mugs of coffee and reading the business sections from newspapers left by tourists, who picked out the fashion and sports sections to take to the beach. As she read the grim economic news, she had only one thought on her mind: "I wish Sabrina would come home soon."

Sabrina and Blair had been childhood friends and knew that one day they would join forces to make their beloved Esperanza even greater—but they weren't sure how. So

Sabrina went off to college in Chicago to learn business, and Blair stayed home to run the only business she knew—making tourists happy with her special Irish coffees, and making townsfolk happy by staying open well into the wee hours.

"I can't wait to get home," Sabrina thought as she sipped her own coffee many miles away from Esperanza. Her school friends were planning summer getaways to the beach, where they could be lazy, forget about reading textbooks, and just soak up the sun. But Sabrina knew her summer at the beach would be invested in working hard to keep Esperanza optimistic, as her friends' parents—and families all over the world—would cancel their vacations as dark economic news began to seep into their anxious nightmares.

Even though half a continent separated them, the same thing was worrying both Blair and Sabrina. They faithfully read the business news and tracked travel trends around the country. They knew that from coast to coast people were canceling vacation plans, opting to be more conservative with their finances. Sabrina and Blair closed their newspapers that morning with a worried sigh. They agreed with the Firebird Bar revelers on one point only: this would be a summer no one would soon forget.

Their suspicions began to take shape the very next morning. A small child looked up from his sand pail and said, "Look Mommy, all the boats have gone away." His mother looked

out into the bay. It wasn't just the boats that had disap-
peared; even the surfers had vanished. Looking over her
right shoulder toward the golf course, she could see that the
golfers had "gone away" too.

Up and down the coast, vacationers were checking out early,
concerned about conserving money. No one lingered for
another round of golf, another wave, or another beach side
cruise. Everyone was leaving.

Chapter Two

The sad beach was empty, but the sand felt wonderful under Sabrina's feet as she ran through the surf, dodging sand-pipers, and struggling to keep up with Blair. She got home late the night before, and this was their first chance to be together and talk about the summer that stretched before them.

"Phyllis told us last night that the Starfish has lost all its bookings through Labor Day," Blair reported. "People only come off the freeway for an hour or two. They take pictures of the beach and then get back in their cars to drive to the city. Everyone talks about the beach like it's a deserted island." Sabrina just listened, breathing hard as they contin-ued on the run she and Blair had been sharing for many years.

"The stores are getting a fraction of their normal business this summer. Amanda has had to lay off all her summer help from the china shop," Blair continued. "Nicholas just shut down his antiques store altogether. He said that if he had the money, he'd take a buying trip to France this summer, but he's afraid to spend the cash."

"The good news is," Blair continued, eyeing her friend's shapeless blonde hair, "you can get a haircut at La Coiffure at a third of the normal price. I'm closing the Firebird in the afternoons now, so I'm free until 5:30."

"This is all backwards," said Sabrina. "The prices are supposed to go up in the summer, not down. And since when did you start taking afternoons off? In the summer you were making beds in the afternoons."

"There are no beds to make."

"How's Concurso doing?" asked Sabrina, mentally measuring Esperanza's decline against its competition.

"Not any better than we are," said Blair. "The only thing it has going for it is the Marine Mammal Research Center, which still has some government funding."

The two ran in silence toward the cliff-top golf course. Even that was abandoned, except for a few grazing mule deer, which leisurely gorged on the overgrown grass. Last summer at this time, the girls would have long since turned around

for fear of being hit by a stray golf ball. Today they could
have run on the course itself.

"Hey! Take a look at that," said Blair as she gazed up at the
cliffs ahead of them.

Sabrina looked in the direction of Blair's stare and spotted a
lone figure picking his way through the boulders and tide
pools. Every now and then he'd stoop down, pick up something out of the still water, examine it, and then gently put it
back.

"I don't recognize him, do you?" asked Sabrina.

"He must be a tourist. Wow, I thought they'd all gone
home," Blair replied.

As they approached him, they could tell he wasn't an ordi-
nary tourist, if he was a tourist at all. He moved around the
unstable crags of the boulders like a graceful dance partner.
When he looked up and spotted them, he didn't fidget or
wave overeagerly as people on vacation sometimes do. He
just stood there as if he owned the beach. Suddenly Blair
felt as though she was the visitor. "I thought all the tourists
had gone home," she said in a friendly but matter-of-fact
way as they approached the young man.

"Have they? I wouldn't know," he said, looking around him

as though noticing for the first time that the beach was deserted. "I just had some time on my hands so I thought I'd come to Esperanza and make a day of it. It's a two-hour drive, even though it's only 75 miles. The coastal highway is gorgeous but it really slows you down."

"You must be from Concurso," Sabrina said. "We were just talking about it. How's business there? From what we hear, you guys are being hit just as hard as we are. And business is the only thing that makes the folks around here happy."

"Yeah, tourism has tanked," he said, "which makes it really hard to get a decent cup of coffee in the mornings. Most of the coffee shops have given up for the summer. Can't say as I blame them, but I was hooked on the spice muffins at Louie's. Now I'm stuck with what I can make myself for breakfast."

"Ah, so you must be with the Marine Mammal Research Center," Blair deduced. "Lucky you! You have a steady paycheck."

"So far, so good," he said with a small chuckle. "Even those funds can dry up if we're not on top of it every time budget season rolls around."

Sabrina had waited for him to volunteer his name, but now decided to get that ball rolling.

"I'm Sabrina and this is Blair. We grew up here," she said.

"I'm Jim D'Artagnan, and I didn't," he said with a smile. "I come from Key West. Most people call me JD."

The women looked at him and thought the same thing: here's another native from a place where people come to pay good money to marvel at 'paradise' and then go home again. Even though he grew up 3,000 miles away from here, the three of them understood they shared a common, realist's perspective of how much work it takes to keep paradise humming.

"D'Artagnan, D'Artagnan, I've heard that name before," said Blair. "Is your father someone famous?"

"Nope," he said. "I get asked that a lot. The famous D'Artagnan was the fourth Musketeer." He spotted the confused look on both their faces, a look he had seen before.

"Most people think there were only three Musketeers, but there were four. D'Artagnan was the youngest. Michael York played him in the old movie with Raquel Welch, remember?"

Whether they did or not, he wasn't certain. They were nodding yes, but they had both crinkled their eyebrows like they were flipping through their memory banks and coming up, well, blank. So he continued: What's cool about D'Artagnan is that he stood for all that stuff about 'all for one and one for all,' teamwork, and self-sacrifice. So when I was old enough to read about him, I thought, 'I want to be just like him.'"

"That's kind of a tall order, isn't it?" asked Blair. "I mean, isn't it easier if you have a big plumed hat, a broad sword, and a horse?"

"I'd probably just cut myself with the sword," JD said, laughing. "Wouldn't mind having the horse, though," he said glancing behind him at the long stretch of beach they had just walked since meeting at the tide pools.

"It's a nice ideal, at any rate," he concluded, turning his face to the ocean's horizon. "That business about self-sacrifice for the sake of a bigger cause is good to remember when I'm seasick out there counting dolphins."

Thrilled to have found the beginnings of a new friendship ("fresh blood" was how Sabrina and Blair put it when they were sure JD was out of hearing distance), the three of them exchanged cell phone numbers and said goodbye at the next rocky point. JD turned around and jogged back to the cliffs. Sabrina and Blair climbed the sandy dunes back up to Ocean Avenue to open the Firebird.

Chapter Three

Three weeks passed, and Blair and Sabrina could see the town sinking quickly into despair. The china store closed. The emerald shop shuttered for the season. At the antiques store, the sign on the door, "Gone to France," told passers-by—had there been any—that the proprietor was replenishing his stock in Provence. In truth, he was visiting his mother in Phoenix. Dave stopped selling T-shirts and was beginning to play with the idea of selling bumper stickers that read "I Survived the Summer From Hell"—strictly for his neighbors and friends, of course—certainly not for the tourist trade. There wasn't any.

Over at the Starfish Bed and Breakfast, Phyllis closed up all but two rooms. At the drugstore, Tom wasn't selling any sunblock. There were no tourists to buy it, and the locals frugally dug up last year's bottles from the back of their cabinets. No point in spending money like it grows on trees.

The only person making money was Blair. People didn't stop going to the Firebird Bar. In fact, they started coming in the mornings now, so Blair extended her "open late at night just for the locals" policy to include most of the day, since the locals were the only customers.

The conversation in the Firebird Bar had changed significantly. Instead of bragging and crowing about what a great season it was going to be, they gradually began blaming one another for the lack of tourism.

"You've overpriced your rooms at the Starfish," Dave said to Phyllis. "If you would lower your rates, people would start coming again."

"You're crazy," she shot back to Dave, pointing a chipped fingernail at him. (Her normally impeccable nails hadn't seen a manicure in weeks). "I'm the only class act in this town. Your tacky T-shirts have made Esperanza look like a tourist trap."

"What are you laughing at?" Phyllis turned to Tom, the drugstore owner. "Since when did you start stocking such cheesy beach stuff? Have you checked the batch code on that sunblock? It looks like it's been on some dollar store shelf since 1985. This town is supposed to be up market, not mass market."

"Oh, right," Tom answered sarcastically, "all the tourists left town because they didn't like my sunblock."

Sabrina, tucked away in a dark corner with just one small light shining on her Wall Street Journal, looked over the top of the paper and caught Blair's eye. With a quick nod of her head toward the door, her message was clear: "Let's close up and get out of here."

Blair leapt into action: "Alright you guys, clear out!" she yelled. "I'm closing up until happy hour—if you can call it that."

Grumbling, the Esperanza crowd didn't even have the spirit to resist Blair's commands. Putting down their spare change as tips, they shuffled out of the door and into the bright sunlight—and empty sidewalks. Up and down the street, the windows of the antiques and art shops were dark. Only Tom's store was open, with yesterday's New York Times still in the stands. Inside, a bored teenager stood by a cash register that had only rung up a roll of antacids all day. Now that the Firebird was closed for the day, everyone was at a loss: "How are we going to kill a whole day now that the bar is closed?"

Sabrina and Blair knew what they were going to do. They were going straight to the beach. They knew that a good run on the sand would clear their minds and boost their spirits. And there was also the special attraction of a possible meeting with their new friend from Concurso.

JD had begun coming to Esperanza more frequently since meeting Sabrina and Blair. He hadn't expected to be so lonely in Concurso when he arrived from Florida. He had been eager to start his career in dolphin research, but everyone there was as obsessed about the politics of their funding sources as the folks in Esperanza were obsessed about tourism—or the lack of it. He missed his girlfriend in Key West, and no one seemed to want to make friends with this newcomer without credentials or powerful political contacts.

Despite the two-hour drive to Esperanza, JD spent much of his spare time there instead of in Concurso, where his colleagues were busy making political connections. When his boss assigned him to the South Bay Quadrant, he was delighted. He was savvy enough to know this assignment was reserved for the non-starters of the group—and since he didn't "play the game," he was firmly designated as a non-essential employee. But he didn't mind. South Bay included Esperanza, which meant he could spend more time there, e-mailing his census reports from his notebook computer. Summer stretched before him, offering the opportunity to do the work he loved. Plus, he was enjoying spending his free time with two new friends.

"Look! There he is, over by the tidal pools!" Blair said as Sabrina was brushing the wind-blown hair out of her eyes and adjusting to the glare from the beach. They had gotten into the habit of searching the shoreline for JD, and many times he'd be there. If he wasn't, they knew they would see him later in the evening at the Firebird, since he had taken to sleeping in Blair's spare back room. "He's a friend from Key West," Blair explained to the bar patrons. "He's doing some research on the beach."

"Hey! Let me put my notebook up on that rock over there, and I'll go for a run with you," he said. The three of them eased into a relaxed jog down the abandoned beach. The grins on their faces were so identical they could have been triplets.

Sabrina was the first to look up from their pounding bare feet. "Hey, what's that? Looks like last night's high tide brought us a present," she said, echoing the tradition of her ancestors who searched the sands and reefs for treasures brought in from shipwrecks.

In the distance, a dark gray lump gleamed dully in the sand, just beyond reach of the surf. As they approached the mystery delivery, the curve of the lump's profile made it clear this was no treasure chest.

"It's a napping seal," Blair off-handedly concluded. But it didn't look furry enough. What was it?

"A beached dolphin, oh gosh!" JD said. "Look how far up the sand it's laying. It must have been here for an hour already!"

Blair and Sabrina stopped in their tracks while JD surged ahead to take a closer look. In three seconds, he had already whipped out his cell phone, flipped it open, and dialed. While he waited for an answer, he looked back to the women and said:

"Fun time's over."

Chapter Four

It's a shame most Esperanzans don't spend much time on their beach. If one of the villagers had been down beneath the dunes, he would have witnessed an unusual moment. Not the beached dolphin—there would be plenty of time to see that very soon. It was the sight of Blair and Sabrina soberly taking orders from the young stranger from Key West.

If you want to negotiate prices with a beer distributor within a breath of his profit margin (and then have him sincerely thanking you for your business), Blair is the one you go to. If it's a business plan you want, Sabrina's mastery of the intricacies of facts and figures is already legend among the professors and venture capitalists lurking in the hallways of the University of Chicago. These two liked to set the agenda, not follow orders.

But there they were, standing stock-still and silent as JD ticked off a list of to-dos like they were learning how to decommission a bomb. Only when he said, "OK, get started!" did they break into a sprint, fly up the steep dunes, and run up the sidewalks of Esperanza in an urgent search for help.

"Me and my big mouth," huffed Blair as her bare feet stepped from the sand onto the hard pavement. "Why did I go and close the bar this morning? Everyone would still be there in one place. Now we have to track them down."

Sabrina was more reasonable. "If you hadn't closed the bar, we wouldn't have gone running and we wouldn't have found the dolphin. JD would have stayed at the far end of the beach and the dolphin would probably have died."

"Shut up."

"I'm just saying…"

"I know. You're right. Shut up anyway."

"You go to the drugstore and the T-shirt shop, since they're right next to each other," Blair suggested. "I'll ask Phyllis to go to the health club, and then I'll open the Firebird."

Within seven minutes most of the regular patrons crowded the Firebird. Tom and Dave were there, wondering why Sabrina had come for them. Phyllis closed the Starfish, then went to the health club and rounded up the guys in the free weights room, who followed her back to the Firebird in a sweaty, red-faced parade. When they all convened, they found the bar's lights strangely bright, with Blair sitting on the bar itself, way up high so she could see—and be seen— by everyone who rallied to this strange all-hands call for help.

Reaching high over her head, she grabbed the braided rope cord dangling from the old ship's bell (a relic from the days when Carl owned the bar) and clanged it with all her might. The noisy room plummeted into a deep hush.

"Okay everyone, listen up!" she said, surprising no one with her customary no-nonsense attitude. "Sabrina, JD, and I just found a dolphin that has beached itself down at the south end, and we've got to get busy!"

"I'll say," said the commissioner of tourism, "this is the best thing that's happened all summer!" He had heard that a recent dolphin rescue far down the coast had helped to rally tourism there.

"No it's not," said Sabrina, who by now was sitting next to Blair on the bar. "This is terrible news. The dolphin could die if we don't do something right now."

"Why don't we just push it out to sea like they did with those whales off Cape Cod?" offered a voice from deep inside the crowd.

"Well, to start with" began Sabrina, "the dolphin isn't like a whale. JD says whales and dolphins beach themselves for different reasons. Dolphins do it because they're sick. They can't just be re-floated and swim away happily. If we send this dolphin back to sea, it will probably die."

"So what can we do?"

Blair jumped in: "There is a dolphin rescue network covering all of the coastal United States. The nearest center is coming to get the dolphin. But, it's going to take a while for them to get here. So in the meantime, we need to do what we can to help."

"Like what?"

"Let's just say we're all in for a long afternoon," said Sabrina. "You guys from the health club, we're going to need your strength to help keep the dolphin upright in the sand. Oh, don't look so confident, just wait until the tide starts coming in and the dolphin begins to thrash."

"Dave and Tom," Blair added, "We're going to need lots of T-shirts and sunblock—the good stuff, Tom, the highest SPF you've got."

"What can I do to help?" piped up Phyllis.

"We've got a very special job for you," Sabrina answered with a sly grin. "Let's just say your next manicure is on the Firebird."

With the meeting adjourned, the townspeople filed down to the dunes of Esperanza's beach.

Chapter Five

The group worked their way down to the beach, with Sabrina and Blair speeding ahead. The guys from the health club (who felt just a little irritated they couldn't keep up with Sabrina and Blair) quickly joined them. After a little break in the crowd, Tom, Dave, and Sam followed, each hoping that no one else could hear their labored breathing. Behind them, Phyllis quietly stifled whimpers as the dried dune grass and twigs scratched her ankles below her Capri pants.

By the time the group broke through the last row of bushes and onto the sand, they saw Blair and Sabrina on their knees on each side of the dolphin, scooping sand away from its motionless body. Their friend JD was slowly walking around the dolphin, carefully studying it from all angles.

"Looks like a tourist inspecting a rental car for dents," Tom thought as he stumbled down the damp slope of sand toward the muscle boys who had already gathered. Besides Sabrina,

Blair, and that JD fellow, no one was really doing much to speak of, except standing around and staring.

When everyone was assembled, JD said: "I want to thank everyone for coming. This is going to take all of us. Now, here's what I want you to do." As he drew in his next breath to speak, Esperanza's mayor interrupted him.

"Maybe we shouldn't be too fast about this. My office is making phone calls right now. Maybe we should give the media a chance to get here."

"Yeah!" Phyllis answered brightly. "And then we'll be known as the town that let this poor creature die on the sand while we stood around waiting for publicity."

Surprised, Sabrina, Blair, and JD slowly pivoted their gaze from each other toward Phyllis. A fresh admiration filled their eyes, and sent her the message "You go, girl!"

JD began once more. "Okay, here's what we need to do: Your job," he said looking directly at the men from the gym, "is to keep the dolphin from hurting itself. That means supporting the dolphin with all your strength and keeping it from breaking away once the tide starts coming in. It's going to get harder and harder as the dolphin starts floating again. It will probably start to thrash and want to break loose."

JD scanned the crowd that had gradually formed a circle around the dolphin. He spotted the man he was looking for.

"It's Tom, right?" The man holding a bin filled with bottles of sunblock nodded his head. "Great! I know it seems weird, but dolphins can get sunburned. So I want you to keep slathering sunblock on the dolphin's back."

"And Dave, thanks for bringing all those T-shirts. After Tom has gone one round with the sunblock, you place wet shirts on the dolphin's skin. That will keep it moist and protected until the rescue truck arrives."

"Be careful not to get any water in the dolphin's blow hole," JD added. "It can drown. Remember, even though they live in the water, dolphins are mammals and they need their airways clear."

Everyone nodded solemnly.

"Now Phyllis, I have an extra special job for you," JD said with a smile. "You may not like it now, but you're going to love it later when Blair makes good on that manicure promise."

Phyllis stepped forward, feeling a mixture of pride at being singled out and a little apprehension about what she was going to be asked to do to earn a manicure. JD took her hand and guided her to kneel with him beside the dolphin's left flipper.

"See these flippers? They're called pectoral fins," JD said. "They're designed to hang down freely in the water. The dolphin uses them to balance and stay upright in the water. With the dolphin resting on the sand like this, there's a tremendous amount of pressure on the fins' skeletal structure. If the fins broke, the dolphin wouldn't be able to swim properly. Right now, there's only one way to protect those fins."

Phyllis didn't need to hear any more. She got to work right away, using both hands to scoop out the sand from around the left fin. When she was done, she crawled on her hands and knees around the dolphin to work on the right fin.

JD stood up and said, "Okay everyone! The good news is: we have everything we need to keep this dolphin alive and safe while we wait for the rescue truck to come. But it's going to take a couple of hours for the truck to get here. So, let's get to work."

Chapter Six

All afternoon Phyllis dug and scraped. The town's strongest men hoisted, lifted, and shifted their own weight to get a better grip on the sand with their toes as the rising tide began to threaten their balance and float the dolphin. JD kept an eye on them and gave each one a break as needed to shake out burning muscles.

Tom drained the 10th bottle of his best sunblock, filling a basket that a neighbor brought down to the beach with the empties. A few neighbors dug around in the back of their cupboards and found bottles of sunblock to donate to the cause because they felt bad about Tom using up his sunblock inventory.

Sabrina stood by, wringing water out of Dave's soaked T-shirts and draping them across the back of the dolphin, which had begun to thrash now that it felt the familiar weightlessness of its body in the water. Dave sent his teenage clerk back to the store for straw and canvas hats for everyone, and she came back with sunglasses too. Dave thanked her for being so thoughtful.

The local Aquifer salesperson spotted the crowd gathered at the beach while driving the cliffside road on his route to deliver bottles of water to his home accounts. "So that's why no one's answering their doorbells—everyone's at the beach," he thought. It didn't take him long to figure out what was going on. He backed his truck down the boat ramp and carried two cases of bottled water to the group.

"Here," he said, "I'll square this with Aquifer later."

Blair, for her part, rounded up a few more townspeople, and together they set up a table filled with pitchers of lemonade and iced tea. Some of the residents in the beach-front houses thought the table still looked a little bare, so they ran back to their houses and returned with a strawberry pie, cookies, and a cake.

Fifteen of the townspeople stood up to their hips in the rising tide. Somewhere in the center of all that humanity was a dolphin, whose only job was to stay as still as possible and wait for the truck. Although Phyllis' job was finished as the dolphin rose off the sand, she didn't leave the group's tight circle.

The chattering group of Esperanzans fell into a concentrated silence as they strained more and more to keep the dolphin under control. Except for the various ringing tones of cell phones left high, protected, and ignored on the rocks, the only sounds on the beach were the waves slapping at thighs and knees—and the sound of the dolphin's tail as it did its own slapping against the water's surface. Every once in a while it would click and whistle quietly to itself, almost like it was humming a little tune to keep itself entertained. It was surprisingly relaxed. As the water rose, this became less and less the humans' territory, and more and more the dolphin's.

After several quiet minutes, JD broke the silence. "Listen everyone, there's something you need to know. The rescue truck I called is the nearest one available. And that means it will be coming from—"

"Concurso!" Phyllis exclaimed. Several of the townspeople looked a little uneasy and a few mumbled "it figures."

"Yeah. The rescue team is part of the Marine Mammal Research Center in Concurso, and I think you should know, I'm part of the Research Center, too."

Folks didn't like the sound of this.

"I didn't mean to deceive anyone," JD quickly added, "and I sure never thought we'd all end up together in a situation like this! I just came to this beach to study dolphins. I know Concurso is in competition with you guys, and things are pretty difficult these days, so I just didn't mention the Research Center."

Blair and Sabrina held their breath, unsure of the townspeople's reaction to this confession.

"Are you really from Key West?" Phyllis asked quietly.

"Yes. Born and bred there. I got assigned to the Concurso center, but after I made some good friends here in Esperanza, I started working from the South Quadrant." He glanced at Blair and Sabrina, who were still looking a bit nervous.

There was a moment of awkward silence, then Phyllis said, "Well, I guess we're lucky you were here today."

"Yeah," said Dave, "we would probably have floated the dolphin back out to sea!"

The townspeople were so focused on processing this information that they didn't hear the rescue truck come to a stop on the firm sand behind them. It had a long, flat bed, filled with poles and a large canvas sling. Tom was the first to see the truck. "It's here!" he yelled.

The truck was already positioned so that its tailgate faced the ocean, and four men dressed in wetsuits were preparing to carry the sling into the surf.

"Hey Rick! Al, you're here too!" JD said. "Phil, and Dan…great! I can't believe you all made it!"

"Hi, JD! Concurso to the rescue!"

With the mention of the name 'Concurso,' the townspeople seemed to explode with one loud, indignant voice. "You!" "I knew it!" "Concurso is going to get all the credit for this!" They glared at JD with new suspicion.

Chapter Seven

The guys from the gym closed in protectively around the dolphin, making it clear with their considerable body language that no one was going to take this dolphin anywhere until a few questions were answered. JD, Blair, and Sabrina each stifled a surge of panic as they calculated the hours the rescue team would need for driving to the Research Center. Time was getting critical, but it was obvious that the rescue team needed the group's permission to remove the dolphin from their control.

The team stood in the water waiting for a definitive signal from JD that it was okay to take over. They had federal jurisdiction, but they didn't feel like that was going to give them any real leverage against angry townspeople.

JD spoke up. "OK, I understand that 'Concurso to the rescue' doesn't sound good to you. But this team is from Concurso, and that is where this dolphin has to go. The

Research Center is the nearest place where it can get the help it needs."

Everyone knew this made sense, but they were still not happy about it. Blair decided to try to dispel their reluctance.

"Look, we've worked hard and I think we've done a great job. But bottom line, this dolphin is a marine mammal. So, what protects it? Anybody?"

"The Marine Mammal Protection Act," murmured a small, voice from deep within the group.

"Right! A free beer goes to whoever it was who spoke up,'" she said. "And who is allowed to work directly with marine mammals?" she coached them.

"Experts authorized by the government," Phyllis volunteered.

"So, I guess we need some people like that, don't we?" Blair responded.

The townspeople turned their eyes towards the four strangers in wetsuits. The town muscle men each caught the eye of a rescue team counterpart. Without exchanging a word, they carefully made room for the team and the canvas sling, amazingly without losing control of the dolphin. JD shook the hand of each Esperanza man who stepped away from the dolphin as the rescue expert took his place. The changing of the guard was flawless, with all egos intact.

As this little drama played itself out, only Sabrina heard the distant sound of yet another motor growing louder as it approached the group on the beach. She also was the first to spot the automobile as it got bigger and bigger as it drew nearer. She didn't recognize it, and that alone spelled trouble. Esperanza was so small, everyone knew everyone's vehicle. As it pulled up to the scene of the rescue, Sabrina's worry was confirmed: this car was from Concurso.

Three men and a woman stepped quickly from the car. One of the men was clearly in charge of this group; another man had a notepad; the third carried a long pole with a fuzzy microphone. The woman hoisted a video camera on her shoulders. The weight of the camera, combined with the instability of the sand under her feet, made her stagger just a little bit. The leader was already talking, gesturing grandly before the camerawoman for what he hoped would be authoritative effect.

"...And so you see the amazing capabilities of the crack Concurso team in rescuing stranded marine mammals off our shores, no matter how remote these locations are. In this case, the dolphin was stranded 75 miles away from our central headquarters, but because we strategically station biologists up and down this rugged coast, we were able to mobilize this rescue instantaneously."

Sabrina, catching the key phrases of this spectacular lecture, thought to herself: "Hmmm, no mention of Esperanza." The townspeople noticed this, too, and were feeling suspicious again.

"Ah, here's our hero now," said the speaker, as JD approached this newly arrived group. "He's been here all day—uh, folks, could you please step aside so this nice young lady can take pictures of the dolphin and the rescue team?"

The speaker then cheerfully turned to face JD: "Hi, JD, I see our carefully designed rescue plan worked smoothly from start to finish today. Good job."

"Hi, Ken. Actually, a lot of the credit goes to—," JD began brightly, but he was cut off mid-sentence as his boss grabbed him by the elbow and roughly moved him out of hearing distance of the small group of journalists.

"What are you trying to do?" Ken hissed. But he kept a smile on his face, as if he were having a friendly chat with one of his employees—just in case that insufferable camerawoman should swing her lens around his way. "This is clearly a Concurso story. If we give Esperanza this publicity

opportunity, Paul at the tourism office will be all over me."
JD wasn't moved. "If it wasn't for the folks here in
Esperanza, we wouldn't have had a dolphin to save," he said,
just as Sabrina was coming up behind him. She overheard
the rest: "Saving a dolphin has its own moral imperatives,
and that's good enough for me. But if you want to turn this
into a media blitz, the benefits should go to these wonderful
people from Esperanza, not the tourism folks in Concurso."

Ken laid out the big picture for JD slowly, as if he was talking to a child, a smile still fixed on his face. "If tourism
doesn't pick up in Concurso, we're not going to have the
resources we need to keep the research center running," he
said with strained patience. "It's my relationships with the
Concurso power brokers that keep us going. So Concurso
has to get the credit. Your attitude makes it clear you're not
the team player I thought I hired. The South Bay census is
almost completed. I'll give you two weeks to finish up, and
then you're done. Unless, of course, you can see your way to
telling these reporters how our fine rescue team has secured
this dolphin's future."

"Forget it," JD said. "The rescue team will take over from
here, but Esperanza's townspeople worked hard to save that
dolphin. I'm going to make sure they get the credit."

At this point, the camerawoman stepped up to the small
group. With a large camera on her shoulders, it was easy for

everyone to overlook the earphones on her head. And with all this excitement, JD's boss completely forgot she had clipped a microphone to his collar before they got into the car in Concurso. One look at her and Ken immediately remembered the microphone and battery pack stuffed in his hip pocket. One word came into his mind as all this dawned on him. But he wasn't about to make matters worse by uttering it aloud.

The camerawoman broke the shocked silence: "Actually, my obligation is to the truth of the story, not Esperanza or Concurso," she said. "JD says the Esperanzans played a big part in this rescue. I'm going to make sure that part of the story gets told."

"And just so you know, Ken," she added, "wrongful termination stories are big with my editor." She turned toward the snack table, the sound man following her, and the twosome began talking to the excited lady with the ravaged manicure.

Epilogue

Blair closed the Firebird for the afternoon just one more time that summer. She knew the tourists would be down at the beach, soaking up the last few days of summer sun, and most of the townspeople would be at the airport. Two weeks had passed since the "Dolphin Incident," as it came to be known, and the dolphin was alive and well.

Life and business in Esperanza were rebounding also. Inspired by the dolphin rescue story, Esperanza's legions of fans began to return. They might stay a couple days less, and buy a few less souvenirs—financial worries were still an issue—but they were back. They might buy the bargain sun-block, or a smaller china figurine, but they were buying. Esperanza's mayor and tourism commissioner worked night and day to keep the dolphin story alive and the publicity flowing.

JD did his part by making appearances on the beach almost every morning, to answer questions and describe the rescue to curious beachgoers. Everyone recognized him from the television news and magazine articles.

Tom, Phyllis, and several other townspeople were likewise enjoying their moment in the spotlight. Phyllis' "name the dolphin" contest was attracting many suggestions; plans were underway for a naming ceremony, and for the dolphin's release back to the sea—right at the spot where it had been rescued.

Now, JD was heading home to Florida. His census was completed and he decided it was time to look for a new assignment closer to home. Blair, Sabrina and many of the townspeople joined him at Esperanza's small airport to say goodbye to their very own local hero.

JD was already dressed in a Key West souvenir T-shirt and shorts and wore big, sporty sandals on his feet. It was as if he had already gone. But Blair and Sabrina knew they'd see JD again. In fact, they had plans to meet in December— this time in Key West, where JD was going to be married.

"Man!" Sabrina had said, when he broke the good news to the girls on one of their daily morning runs, "When you make a stand, there's no stopping you. What'll be next? I can't even imagine."

"Here," said Blair as she thrust a business card into JD's hand. "I thought it was time for a change. The bar has been called the Firebird long enough."

JD looked down and saw Blair's name and phone number. That was familiar. The rest was completely different—a new logo of a dolphin leaping high into the air. "And what's this—a new name?"

"Say it out loud," Blair said. "I need to hear it again and again to make it sink in."

JD took a deep breath to calm his welling emotions and uttered the new name of Blair's tavern:

"JD Dolphin's!"

"Yes," Blair sighed with a satisfied smile. "That was definitely the right thing to do."

SECTION THREE
Lessons Learned

The Seven Principles of
The D'Artagnan Way

PRINCIPLE ONE

Commit to a Shared Dream

In Esperanza, the townspeople were faced with a devastating drop in tourism, and therefore in their economy. Instead of supporting each other, they ended up blaming one another for their collective misfortune. It seemed that the cohesive and harmonious lifestyle Esperanza was famous for could be maintained only in prosperous times.

But when a shared objective presented itself, they rallied around one vision: helping to save a stranded dolphin's life. The townspeople were willing to put aside their individual self-interest for this cause—even if it meant discomfort and sacrifice. The unifying experience had a profound effect on them all.

How do you commit to a shared dream, when it seems as though everyone is absorbed in short-term self-interest at the expense of the long-term health and well being of the group?

These are the essential steps for inspiring everyone to focus on a single unifying cause.

Get to know your team and your own skills.
The skills and expertise of your team members is your greatest asset. Leverage them creatively and wisely, and there's no limit to what can be achieved. Each person within a group brings a unique skill or talent to the cause. In Esperanza, Sabrina and Blair brought their leadership talents and business acumen; Dave and Tom, the merchants, had valuable products in stock; Phyllis had her passion and need to be helpful; even the men at the gym had a valuable strength. And of course, JD had his knowledge of marine mammals. Taken separately, none of these gifts would have been sufficient. But used strategically, these aptitudes were just the right tools to achieve the objective of saving the dolphin.

Establish clear goals and set priorities.
All the talent, energy, and knowledge in the world may not solve the problem without a focused sense of mission and purpose. Decide what you want to achieve, and aim for that desired result with clear vision. Distinct parameters help to make a goal approachable. Everyone on the beach wanted to save the dolphin, but JD established the priorities that would allow them to achieve this goal: keep the fins safe, prevent the dolphin from thrashing, protect the skin from sunburn. By defining these priorities JD was able to keep the group focused on the mission.

Clarify performance requirements of team members.
Leadership requires explicit command, especially when you're
in charge of a large group of passionate people. In the
Esperanza story, everyone had a role in "saving the day."
Each team member understood their role and the specific
tasks that were required of each of them. This clarity kept
them focused on achieving the planned outcome.

Choose accountability over acceptance.
Leadership, even when everyone agrees on the desired objective, can come at a cost to your own personal needs. It is
important to remain accountable to the mission, even if this
requires unpopular choices. At the beginning of the dolphin
rescue, JD enjoyed an attitude of acceptance from the
Esperanzans and from his boss, Ken. Through the course of
the day, that acceptance was placed in serious danger several
times. But JD remained focused on his mission, and made
decisions according to what was best for that mission. Each
choice carried a potential price he might have to pay, but his
own interests were set aside for the greater good.

Challenge team member expectations.
When leading a group of people toward a shared goal, you
must inspire them to expand their idea of what's possible—
especially as compared to their current situation. As the
Esperanza story began, high expectations for the summer
shattered in response to dark economic forecasts. The
townspeople must revise their expectation to survival, a shift

that nearly tore the community apart. The beached dolphin challenged their expectations once again, bringing them back together in unexpected ways that ultimately yielded economic benefit.

Follow-up and follow through.
Commit to win/win! In The D'Artagnan Way, when a group dedicates its energy and passion toward a shared mission, there is never a loser—even if the outcome doesn't directly benefit each individual. In a group effort, everyone must be committed for the long haul, even when it becomes uncomfortable or expensive. At the end of the adventure, the rewards often extend far beyond the immediate satisfaction of 'mission accomplished.' When the dolphin was picked up by the Concurso rescue team, the Esperanzans faced the possibility of losing credit for their hard work; but their goal was not to receive credit—it was to save the dolphin. They accomplished their mission successfully, and achieved the win they had committed to; getting credit and publicity was a reward beyond their expectations.

Encourage passion for a common purpose.
It is amazing what can be accomplished by an impassioned group focused on a compelling mission. Blair, Sabrina and JD were able to inspire the Esperanzans to commit to the dolphin's survival. The group dedication achieved a goal beyond anything they could have accomplished separately.

Does your team share a defined dream? Is each member committed to it, even if it means that individual benefits may be sacrificed for the greater good? Think about your team's shared goal and identify the reasons why it's important to commit to that goal. Talk about what it means to you individually and as a team to make this dream come true. Take a moment to renew your collective commitment to the shared objective. And then commit to achieving it! The struggle toward the goal becomes easier when you know and trust that people with the same vision are backing you.

PRINCIPLE TWO
Create Strategic Alliances

JD, Blair, and Sabrina began forming their strategic alliance the first day they met on the beach. They didn't realize it at the time, of course, but the pieces were in place for a core group of talent and contacts that ultimately saved the life of the stranded wild dolphin. They thought the alliance would give them the companionship they each needed to survive that dreary summer, not knowing how truly valuable the alliance would prove to be.

Powerful alliances come into our lives through a variety of avenues—some by lucky chance, others through careful planning. Their value is not always obvious in the beginning. Creative management of those alliances will facilitate the achievement of your objectives. Here are some keys to forming and using strategic alliances.

Build personal relationships.
Move beyond the isolation that can come with a leadership

role. When JD, Sabrina, and Blair met on the beach, each of the three had the potential for being a strong leader. JD had knowledge and experience with marine mammals. Sabrina had the advantage of the leadership skills she was learning at the university. And Blair had the strong personality necessary to manage the town's most popular gathering place.

As individuals, they each could have leveraged their leadership skills to make a difference that day—but with limited effect. As a threesome, they made a powerful team that could transform the townspeople into a community of dedicated team members. But to build and leverage this combined power, the three of them needed the personal relationships they had developed with one another.

Learn from others.
(friends, peers, business associates, and strangers)
It is said that knowledge is power. If we pay attention to the expertise and experience of those around us, we enhance our own effectiveness. Blair and Sabrina are on their way to forming a powerful business team, because they are willing to share their skills and knowledge with one another. The townspeople were able to save the dolphin's life because they were willing to learn from JD.

Draw from the support and skills of your closest circles.
Think about your friends and co-workers. What skills do

they possess that might help to further your cause? Each Esperanzan had something to contribute to saving the dolphin's life, and each person wanted to make that contribution. When you are passionate about a goal, friends and colleagues are often inspired to provide advice, support, and help to achieve that goal. It is amazing how much you can accomplish with a little help from the people around you.

Strategic alliances work both ways. Consider and be aware of how your ideas and assistance could help friends and colleagues to achieve their goals. Can your friends and co-workers call on you for your support and skills?

The ideas and talents of each individual are the basis of your strategic alliances. Alliances can be useful when networking to find a new job—or installing a dimmer switch. While you may have almost everything you need to realize your ambitions for a better life and career, maximize your potential by drawing from the abilities and passions of your team.

PRINCIPLE THREE
Respect Each Other's Differences

We may quickly dismiss potential friendships because we prematurely conclude "we don't have anything in common with them." But more often than not, it's good if our friends are different from us. We each bring unique gifts to the table. How useful would those gifts be if they were all the same? It would be like getting 20 toaster ovens for wedding presents.

In principle, it's easy to agree that respecting each other's differences is good and right. But in actual practice, it can sometimes try your patience and test your ability to tolerate different points of view. It can be difficult to sustain receptivity when another person's attitude seems to threaten your own. Consider the various aspects of respect among team members:

Value each member of your team as a human being.
Sometimes we are tempted to regard people in the context of

their jobs, their attitudes, their backgrounds, or other limiting categories. Depending on our attitudes toward those particular categories, we either welcome them into our life or reject them. But people aren't categories; they're individual human beings, each one fully dimensional, with both flaws and talents. And they will often surprise you, if given half the chance. Take Phyllis, for example. Some people might dismiss her as a brassy innkeeper who is mainly interested in her own gain. But she didn't think twice about using her expensively manicured fingernails to dig out the sand to protect the dolphin's fins. Initial assessments rarely reveal a person's true nature and motivation.

Value each team member's strengths, potential for doing good, and skill sets.
When leading a team of impassioned people, it is most productive to assign them to tasks well suited to their abilities. When JD, Blair and Sabrina discovered the dolphin, JD knew it was best to send Blair and Sabrina to recruit helpers—because these two women had lifelong relationships with the townspeople and were trusted by them. Sabrina and Blair knew exactly who would be the best choice for each task. And by the time they had everyone gathered, they had specific assignments for each of the regulars of Blair's tavern. Everyone was valuable and everyone had an exclusive responsibility. Teamed together, they brought a powerful combination of skills and talents to the task at hand.

Broaden team member capabilities.
People don't know the extent of their capabilities until
they're put to the test. Just as muscles are strengthened when
used just beyond their capacity, so are people. On the day
the dolphin beached itself, the townspeople engaged their
skills and abilities in new ways. As a team, stretched beyond
previous limits, they found new strength.

**Encourage team members to express differences of opinion
openly—and create the forum for doing so without fear of
retribution.**
Allowing your team members to speak their mind is the ultimate expression of trust and respect. Many ideas are
improved, and many problems solved, in the course of
healthy debate. Team members who feel free to express concerns and disagreements are less likely to harbor resentments
that can slow the team down.

**Focus on earning respect and commitment, not affection,
from your team.**
It's often difficult for natural leaders (who are typically caring
human beings) to give up the dream of being loved as they
lead. Affection may come, but respect is essential. JD knew
the Esperanzans might not like him when they found out
about his connection to Concurso. But it wasn't important
for them to like him—he needed their respect and commitment to the cause of saving the dolphin. Because of his
expertise concerning the dolphin, and later his willingness to

sacrifice his job, he earned their respect. And, when all was said and done, he won their trust and affection too.

Promote empathy and understanding.
A common passion will unite even the most diverse group of people. When we can set aside our personal concerns and enter into a shared universe focused on something beyond ourselves, we enter a realm where we can put our full potential into action. At the sight of the wild dolphin's helplessness, each Esperanzan, regardless of what his or her own apprehensions may have been, was able to rise above personal limitations and motivations to take part in a greater mission.

When you consider all of the different people you know, think about the valuable potential in their uniqueness. Remember the importance of diverse skills and viewpoints when assembling a team dedicated to an important cause.

PRINCIPLE FOUR
Maintain a Positive Attitude

Even with the best team and the most powerful commitment, the final outcome may remain uncertain until long term results are shown. In these situations, do not allow yourself to sink into negativity. Work to keep your spirits up, and encourage positive thinking among your team.

Emphasize the positive.
When you're making progress, focus on what you have accomplished, not the challenges that are still ahead. Focus on what is going well; be upbeat and optimistic. When JD's connection to Concurso was met with some indignant responses, he remained focused on the task at hand and reinforced the commitment made by the townspeople to save the dolphin.

Look for better ways to get things done.
The team spirit promoted by the philosophies of The D'Artagnan Way indicates that many hands dedicated to a

shared goal will result in successful achievement. When Blair, Sabrina, and JD came upon the dolphin, they might have looked only to each other to solve the problem, avoiding the argumentative townspeople. But they realized they would need more people and tools to ensure the best outcome. There is almost always more than one way to get things done, and it often involves help from more people. The quest for the best approach is part of a positive attitude that can find a solution for almost any problem.

Commit yourself to the objective; then figure out how to achieve it.

The most powerful people begin a challenge by simply assuming they will succeed. With that assumption, the steps toward accomplishing their goal fall more easily into place. Everyone involved in the dolphin rescue understood that losing the sick dolphin back to the waves was simply not an option. Failure should be excluded from your range of possible outcomes. Decide the objective will be achieved, then continue to work towards it, even if methods and means have to be adjusted along the way.

PRINCIPLE FIVE
Choose to Trust

When the Esperanzans spent their time and energy caring for the dolphin, only to discover that they were waiting for a rescue team from their rival village Concurso, they questioned the trustworthiness of young JD. Until they decided to trust that JD was dedicated to saving the dolphin above all other allegiances, they were at risk of blocking the achievement of their shared goal.

Choose trust over suspicion.
This may be tremendously difficult, especially when the situation is not looking good for your team members. The Esperanzans discovered that help was coming in the form of their archrival—and that rival was positioned to get all the credit—and their leader was on their rival's payroll! Their suspicion was natural, but they chose to trust JD for the sake of the dolphin. JD's motives proved to be sincere—he was truly committed to the team and the goal.

Once you have entered into an alliance with a team, stay
true to your word, and choose to trust that your team members
will do the same.

Choose trust for the sake of a larger mission.
Once an alliance is formed for the sake of a greater cause,
personal interests and concerns take a back seat to the goals
of the team. The farther toward the goal the team has progressed,
the more you have to lose by indulging in trivial suspicions
or accusations. The Esperanzans were unhappy to
learn about JD's Concurso connection, but by that time they
were deeply committed to the dolphin rescue, and chose to
see it through in spite of their doubts.

Choose trust unless justified not to.
Followers of The D'Artagnan Way know that their challenge
to trust is not a dare to be foolish. Choose your trusted
partners wisely, based on the skills and talents they bring to
your shared mission. When possible, choose those with a
reputation for commitment to team goals in previous circumstances.
In spite of the commitment to choose trust, if a
team member's actions are consistently contrary to your
shared mission and values—even when given opportunities
to regain your confidence—you may choose to replace them
with someone you know you can count on.

PRINCIPLE SIX
Do the Right Thing

In pursuit of a compelling goal, there may be times when you make sacrifices for a greater good—the right thing— even though it may come at a cost.

The townspeople did the right thing and surrendered the dolphin to the rescue team from Concurso—even though Concurso would probably get the publicity and credit for their work. They understood they might have to give up any expectation of personally benefiting from their sacrifice.

JD was not satisfied with that outcome; in addition to saving the dolphin, he wanted to do the right thing with regard to the Esperanzans, making sure they received the publicity and credit they deserved. He knew when he disagreed with his boss from Concurso that he might be putting his job on the line. But it was the right thing to do, so he took the risk.

How can you consistently do the right thing when security, safety, even pride may be at risk?

Practice sound ethics.
Deep in our hearts, we all know what is right and wrong. The primary question is: do we have the courage and stability to make the right choice when we know we may have to pay a high price for it? The potential exists in each of us for making the right choice even when that choice is difficult. But that strength of courage must be exercised regularly to keep ethical practices sharply focused.

Deal with disrespect.
JD's boss treated him disrespectfully, even threatening him in a public setting. This kind of treatment can erode anyone's self-esteem. And when self-esteem is diminished, the commitment to stay true to your principles is also threatened. However, rising above disrespectful treatment—as JD chose to do—maintains personal dignity and places your self-esteem beyond the reach of small-minded individuals who assume they have power over you and what you do. Stay committed to your values and principles, and make your choices about dealing with disrespect accordingly.

Lead by example.
By standing by the Esperanzans in the end, JD showed his new friends loyalty. But his leadership examples began earlier in the day, when he stayed all day with the townspeople,

guiding the care of the dolphin. He was faithful to his mission, and did not waver in the face of dissent or opposition. He told the truth about his Concurso connection, even though it could compromise the rescue. His actions throughout the rescue were a demonstration of doing the right thing. Be aware that people around you are watching your behavior, and those you lead are learning from your actions. What legacy do you want to leave by your example?

How far will you go to do the right thing? It is natural to be worried and even afraid about your security when you stand up for what you know is right. But when you do the right thing, any negative results can be overcome, and the positive rewards of your commitment to what is right will prevail.

PRINCIPLE SEVEN
Celebrate Success

When the dolphin was safely on its way to the Research Center, and all of the press people had left the beach, JD joined the townspeople of Esperanza in a celebration at Blair's bar. They reminisced about the day's struggles and victories, and in this hour of relaxed camaraderie, the bonds of teamwork that began earlier in the day became even more solid.

Too often, we forget to enjoy a "victory lap" after achieving great deeds. However, this is an important part of the mission. Business leaders must remember to take the time for a victory lap, and encourage the whole team to enjoy it with us.

Keep your eyes on the prize.
Throughout the entire effort, make sure your team is committed to the victory, not to the struggle. When the struggle itself is all-encompassing, it is easy to forget what you are

striving to achieve. Try to stay focused on the goals you are
working for, and celebrate the accomplishment of each goal.

Thank the doers and reward the successes!
Acknowledge the efforts and contributions that made success
possible. Individual achievements are important, even
though the group effort is the ultimate engine for success.

Take time to celebrate success—don't simply dust off your
hands and move on to the next battle. The victory lap is
most productive when it is a team celebration. As the leader,
making certain this happens is part of your job.

SECTION FOUR
Conclusion

The dolphin rescue had a lasting impact on Esperanza and its people. For one afternoon, the group of individual townspeople was unified by the shared experience of saving a life, which altered their relationships and economic outlook in a profound and enduring way.

Saving the dolphin was the goal that day on the beach of Esperanza. It did not matter how many people were required. It did not matter how many hours it took for the Concurso rescuers to get there. It did not matter that JD might lose his job for the sake of the Esperanzans. All that mattered was that the dolphin be rescued, properly cared for, and ultimately returned to the sea where it could live a healthy life in its natural environment.

What is your objective? You will be able to meet it with the help of a spirited team, each person equally committed to achieving the chosen outcome.

Once you experience the exhilarating rush of doing something beyond your expectations, there is no going back. You will be so inspired by your own success and that of your team, you will want to live your life and fulfill your career on a bigger scale. Don't be surprised if every member of your team develops a strong appetite for new achievements and looks for new ways to contribute!

The townspeople of Esperanza remember JD every time they walk under the new sign that hangs over Blair's door. And they mentally send good wishes to Key West, where he is happily married and fulfilled in his work studying Atlantic Bottlenose dolphins off the coast of southern Florida.

Word has it that Phyllis, Dave, and Tom have taken official courses in dolphin rescue. They drove to the Research Center in Concurso to do it. Phyllis was overheard at JD Dolphin's the other day saying "It was the right thing to do."

PRINCIPLES OF THE D'ARTAGNAN WAY

Commit to a Shared Dream

Create Strategic Alliances

Respect Each Other's Differences

Maintain a Positive Attitude

Choose to Trust

Do the Right Thing

Celebrate Success

About the Authors

HARVEY A. MEIER, Ph.D., CMC, is a certified management consultant and president of the Harvey A. Meier Co., a Pacific Northwest management consulting firm. Dr. Meier has worked with hundreds of CEOs, boards, and senior executives of companies of all sizes in a wide range of industries and business sectors to build strong teams, working relationships, and communications. He also is founder and executive director of the Institute for Future Leaders, a training and education organization created to ensure that key managers are well prepared to advance to higher levels of leadership and decision making authority in line with their company's succession planning efforts. And, he serves as a board member of private companies and nonprofit organizations. Before founding his consultancy, Meier held management and executive positions with the former First Interstate Bank of Los Angeles (now Wells Fargo) and with the former Spokane Bank for Cooperatives (now CoBank/Spokane). He co-founded a high-tech start-up sold to a public company and has served as CEO of a privately held distribution company in Silicon Valley.

Dr. Meier has published numerous articles throughout his professional career and has taught at Oregon State University. He has a Ph.D. from The Ohio State University. He and Larry A. Bauman are co-founders of the D'Artagnan Network, a group of independent certified management consultants committed to practicing the D'Artagnan Way. These practices exemplify the principles of unselfish teamwork, collaboration, and inspiration with truth, honor, and integrity in serving the needs of their respective clients.

Harvey lives with his wife, Susan, in Spokane, Washington. You can reach him at the Harvey A. Meier Co. web site www.harveymeier.com, or at harvey@harveymeier.com.

LARRY A. BAUMAN, Ph.D., CMC, is president of Phoenix Business Consulting, Inc., which provides strategic planning, special projects, product sourcing, and sales training to a diverse client base both domestically and internationally.

Before launching Phoenix Business Consulting, Inc., he was senior vice president of sales for Crescent Cardboard, a specialty paper laminator, managing all sales for three business units with 84 independent and company salespeople, seven sales managers, and worldwide customer service at eight locations in the United States and Europe.

Bauman also is co-founder, with Harvey Meier, of the D'Artagnan Network. He is the author of a monthly management newsletter called The Bauman Bizness Bulletin, which is distributed to 10,000 readers. Bauman has written numerous articles and three books on sales strategy entitled Sales Made Easy: 62 Strategies that Work, The Selling Game: Making the Right Moves, and Counting Your Wins: Sales Strategies for Sales Management.

He currently serves on the Chicago IMC Board of Directors as executive vice-president and holds the designation of CMC (Certified Management Consultant). He is a graduate of Emory University, and recently earned a Ph.D. in the field of Behavioral Economics from Rushmore University.

Larry lives with his wife, Beth, in Chicago, Illinois. He can be reached at the Phoenix Business Consulting web site www.bauman.biz, or at larry@bauman.biz.

CORPORATE TRAINING AND CLASSROOM USE

A special price can be arranged for multiple copies of this book for corporate training and college classroom use. Please contact Columba Publishing at 800-999-7491, 330-836-2619 or Larry Bauman (Phoenix Business Consulting) at larry@bauman.biz.

Columba Publishing Company, Inc.
2003 West Market St.
Akron, OH 44313
www.columbapublishing.com